detox

MW00897133

TABLE OF CONTENTS

ABOUT THE AUTHORS

Dr. Jackie Roese grew up in a pagan family in upstate New York. Shortly after coming to Christ, she and her husband Steve moved to Texas to attend Dallas Theological Seminary. Seminary was Jackie's first exposure to Christians, the Bible and the South! After several years of learning, she was brought under the mentorship Dr. Sue Edwards where she was taught to write Bible study materials and teach the Scriptures.

Over the past eight years, she has served as the Teaching Pastor to Women at Irving Bible Church in Irving, Texas. She has taught the Scriptures and trained other women to do the same. In addition, she has envisioned, written and overseen the development of a decade of Bible study materials.

In 2010, Jackie graduated with her Doctorate in Preaching from Gordon Conwell Seminary. It is her desire that women know Jesus through his Word and, in doing so, become more whole as a result. She has a passion to give laywomen the opportunity to develop their teaching skills. From that desiring Jackie felt called to birth The Marcella Project; to transform women to be critical spiritual thinkers and effective teachers of God's Word. Through this ministry women will be challenged to become critical spiritual thinkers about issues pertenent to women, such as body image, sexuality, roles of men and women and more. Along with teaching, writing and training, Jackie also speaks around the U.S. at conferences and retreats.

Jackie resides in Coppell, Texas with her husband, Steve and their three children: Hunter, Hampton and Madison.

ACKNOWLEDGEMENTS

Special thanks to the WE staff at IBC: Julie Pierce, Nila Odom, and Sara Taylor, for their insight, encouragement, expertise, and support, and to Brie Engeler, who contributed her expertise in editing. Dennis Cheatham and Ron Hall were instrumental in design and production. God's best work is done in teams, and this study guide is the result of a collaborative effort. We are grateful for each of you.

WHAT IS THE MARCELLA PROJECT?

The Marcella Project exists to transform women into critical spiritual thinkers & excellent teachers of God's Word.   Our Vision is to create a relevant, valued, empowered & enlightened spiritual community of women.   We are committed to: Teaching God's Word, Creating a community of believers who think critically about theology, practice and women's spirituality, Preparing women to effectively teach God's Word, Promote women to think critically of theology and practice, Prepare women to teach confidently, and to Proclaim God's Word with relevancy

WHO IS MARCELLA?

Marcella was a woman born 325 AD into a wealthy family in Rome. She became a widow seven months after her marriage. Breaking with convention, she never remarried despite several wealthy suitors' proposals. Her faith drove her to long for simplicity, perhaps even an ascetic lifestyle, yet she chose to honor her mother by living with her in her mansion until she died. She brought many young women into their home to be mentored in the Word and she lived a life of service to the poor.

When St. Jerome, who translated the Scriptures into the Latin Vulgate, came to settle in Rome. Marcella quickly approached him to allow her to become his apprentice. He resisted; she persisted. Jerome finally gave in and Marcella became one of his most capable students and a close confidante. Marcella was known to challenge Jerome's theology more than once. It is said he changed his writings on the words 'amen' and 'alleluia' due to Marcella's theological challenges. When Jerome traveled, he would tell those needing instruction in the Word of God to seek out Marcella.

After her mother's death, Marcella moved out of the mansion and gave her wealth away to those in need. When the barbarians invaded Rome, they captured Marcella and beat her in hopes of getting her to give them her money. They didn't believe her when she explained she had none. After long beatings and no success, they released her. Shortly after, she died as a result of those beatings.

Marcella epitomizes what it means to not succumb to the world's ideal of "what it meant to be a woman," but instead chased after Jesus, letting his love define who she would be. She let nothing get in her way of her pursuit to know God through the Word and to live like Jesus by caring for the poor. Her story challenges us to be "Marcella's" in our world, pursuing Jesus at all costs, even if it means defying our world's ideal of womanhood by allowing our love for Jesus to define who we will be and how we will live.

THE ART OF *DETOX*

The first time I heard the word *detox* as a title for this study, images rushed through my mind. And how couldn't they? You can't ignore a strong term like that. Initially, I created covers and imagery that hearkened of scrubbing: broad strokes that depicted the revealing of what's beneath as the result of hard work and determination. But while the process of detoxification is one of long-suffering, the teaching team stressed to me that it's also about hope. And that discussion birthed the art you see today.

The wheat field image is a great choice for *detox* because of its simplicity. It *feels* quiet, uncluttered, hopeful. While the edges of the photo are dark in color there's light in the distance, like dawn, that emulates the purposeful life that detox brings. I chose an image that was organic, as it resembles an escape from the daily tasks and challenges we all face. In all, the imagery suggests the hope of what's beyond the important process of *detox*.

– Dennis Cheatham
Art Director

WHY *DETOX*?

A while back, the staff at IBC enjoyed a lunchtime conversation with several leaders of women from around the country. Musicians, theologians, seminary students, Bible teachers, and leaders of women's ministry were present. These were strong, gifted, and confident women! As we sat around chatting about the normal stuff women in ministry talk about, one woman asked a very intriguing question. She said, "You travel all over the country ministering to women. What do you see today's women struggling with the most?"

To my surprise, the conversation moved quickly to discuss the desperate struggles we all go through as women. We discovered a common thread among these women, who had never gathered together before this moment. We all agreed that women are not able to fully be themselves, for a variety of reasons. We talked about how people-pleasing gets in our way; how women don't see themselves as theological thinkers; and how women who aren't "traditional" find it difficult to fit into the church culture. As I listened to these gifted, confident women, I realized that these issues—insecurity, people-pleasing, a desire to be accepted, fear, and so on—are part of every one of us. I ached for women, all women, to be free to be who God made them to be. For that to happen, we would have to go to God's Word and discover what he says to us about these toxic struggles.

It is my longing that we would address the toxins in our lives that keep us from being ourselves and that keep others who aren't like us from being themselves. What might be accomplished for the Kingdom if we all became comfortable with ourselves and with others! I want to be a woman who is free to be myself and therefore able to accept you as you are. I want to be there for you. I need for you to be there for me. *Detox: Clearing the Way to Spiritual Wellness* was birthed to help us become this type of woman . . . a woman who is fully herself, fully who God intended her to be.

– Jackie Roese
The Marcella Project

HOW TO USE THIS STUDY GUIDE

Women today need Bible study to keep balanced, focused, and Christ-centered in their busy worlds. The study questions in this guide allow you to choose the study level that fits your lifestyle. To provide even more flexibility, you may choose a different level each week depending on your schedule.

> The "core" questions (designated by 1, 2, 3, etc.) require about an hour and a half of weekly study time, yet provide a basic understanding of the text. For busy women, this level offers in-depth Bible study with a minimum time commitment. All students are asked to complete the core questions. Most core questions will be covered in your small-group discussion time.

> The "tool time" sections are designed to help you learn how to use Bible study tools such as a Bible dictionary, concordance, or map.

> The "digging deeper" questions require outside resources such as a Bible atlas, Bible dictionary, and concordance. This will challenge you to learn more about the history, culture, and geography of that time period. You will also be looking up parallel passages for additional insight. These questions may also help you to grapple with complex theological issues and differing views. You are encouraged to investigate deeper by using an interlinear or comparative Greek-English Bible and *Vine's Expository Dictionary* on your own. Some with teaching gifts and an interest in advanced academics will enjoy exploring further.

Choose a realistic level of Bible study. You may want to finish the "core" level first, and then tackle the others as time permits. Take time to savor the questions, and don't rush through the application. The key is consistency.

Whatever level you choose, make your Bible study top priority. Consider spacing your study throughout the week so that you can take time to ponder and meditate on what the Holy Spirit is teaching you. If you are participating in a group study, ask God to enable you to attend meetings faithfully. Come with an anticipation to learn from others and a desire to share yourself and your journey. Give it your best. God promises to join you on this adventure that can change your life.

GUIDELINES FOR GROUP DISCUSSION

1. Come to group study sessions prepared and on time. You will offer more, and you won't miss anything.

2. Respect the value of other women's answers. Listen thoughtfully. Do not expect the leader to correct someone you think has a "wrong" answer. If you have a different opinion, express it graciously.

3. Help others feel safe in speaking up.

4. Focus on the passage being studied.

5. Do you tend to talk too much? Consider marking ahead of time the questions on which you wish to speak. If you are talking more than anyone else, use restraint. Give others a chance to participate.

6. Do you seldom speak up? Offer input early in the discussion. Once you begin to participate, you will feel more comfortable. Your insights and experiences are valuable. Allow others to benefit from what only you can offer.

7. Are you here primarily for fellowship? Our relational needs are important, so time for fellow-ship is built into the study. However, studying God's Word is also a priority and the reason many women are attending. If you desire more fellowship, consider contacting group members outside of class or plan to arrive early.

8. Are you here primarily for Bible study? That's great! Just remember that other women would treasure your friendship and your encouragement. Time spent sharing life experiences, prayer requests, and praying together will enrich your life too.

9. Keep all personal contact information and sharing confidential.

10. Please do not talk about politics or speak critically about other churches.

11. Please do not use the study for sales purposes.

12. Above all, have fun! Delight yourself in the Lord and in his women.

Lesson One

FEAR

Selected Scriptures

We live in a dangerous, unstable, and sometimes violent world. Terrorists crash planes into skyscrapers; hurricanes wipe out whole cities; crazed gunmen open fire on defenseless students.

Our natural tendencies are to run for safety or to hunker down and try to ride it out . . . hoping against hope that we, and the people we love, will be safe. But is that all God has called us to do? To seek safety? Hardly. Pastor Erwin McManus says, "We . . . are called to a path filled with uncertainty, mystery, and risk" (35).

Jesus never promised that life would be free from danger. In fact, he warned his disciples that "in this world [they would] have trouble" (John 16:33). Simply living is risky, and living as a follower of Christ is even more dangerous. After all, his life, the life of our Savior and Master, led to the cross—to suffering and death. And if we truly seek to emulate him, we must be willing to endure the consequences (see Matthew 20:22–28; Luke 9:23).

So, how can we deal with the fear and worry that threaten to grab us by the throat and turn us into cowards? How can we become confident, courageous women who are willing to take risks, trusting that in the process we will become stronger and more mature? The answer is simple but monumental. We have to deliberately face our fears, trusting wholly in the immense and abiding love of Jesus. His "perfect love drives out fear" (1 John 4:18).

UNDERSTANDING FEAR

1. Look up the word *fear* in the dictionary. Now, summarize the definition in your own words. What are a few other words we use to describe *fear*?

 Look up the word *worry*. How are fear and worry different? Try to come up with at least five specific differences.

2. More than 125 times, the Bible tells us *not* to be afraid (see Joshua 8:1; Proverbs 3:25; Mark 6:50; and so on). Read each of the following verses. In each one, what are we specifically told *not* to fear?

   a. Deuteronomy 20:1–4

   b. Proverbs 3:25–26

   c. Isaiah 51:7

d. Matthew 6:31–34

e. Revelation 2:10

3. Why do you think God encourages his people not to be afraid of these things? (See Deuteronomy 31:6; Matthew 28:20; Romans 8:15; 2 Timothy 4:5–8.) Be sure to list at least three reasons.

THE EFFECTS OF FEAR

4. Read the following verses. Then, in your own words, explain some of the negative effects or dangers of living in fear.

a. Proverbs 12:25

b. Jeremiah 1:4–8

c. Mark 4:35–41

5. Have you experienced some of these negative effects in your own life? If so, how did they hinder your spiritual growth? Be candid.

6. Match each Scripture with the type of fear it describes.

____ Adam and Eve (Genesis 3:6–10)   A. Fear of accusation

____ Moses (Exodus 3:11, 4:1, 11, 13)   B. Fear of dying

____ The disciples (Mark 4:35–41)   C. Fear of retaliation

____ Peter (Mark 14:66–72)   D. Fear of punishment

____ Jacob (Genesis 27:41; 32:6–8)   E. Fear of failure

7. What is your greatest fear? How has it manifested itself in your life? Why do you think you struggle with this particular fear?

THE BIBLICAL CONCEPT OF FEAR

NOTE: Fear is referred to in the Bible several hundred times. The Hebrew root word most often associated with fear in the Old Testament—occurring 435 times—is the verb *yara*, meaning "to fear, honor." The related noun, *yir'ah*, can be translated as "fear, worship." In the New Testament, the concept of fear is most often associated with the verb *phobeo*, which means "to fear, reverence, or respect" (Holman 562).

According to the Nelson Study Bible,

> The use of [the word *fear* in Scripture] does not imply that one needs to be afraid of God, but it does demand the appropriate recognition and respect for God's fearsome qualities, such as His righteous wrath (see Ps. 5:4–7). Perhaps somewhat ironically, fear of God leads to confidence in this life, for if we have submitted to the Almighty we do not have to fear any power in this world. (1059)

8. Read 1 Samuel 12:24 and Psalm 27:1. Who or what should we fear most?

Using a concordance or other Bible study tool, search for verses that use the phrase "fear of the Lord." Web sites like www.biblestudytools.net or www.biblegateway.com have features that make this type of research easy. After reading these verses, briefly summarize what you have learned.

Now, considering what the Bible says about fear, how would you counsel a woman who's struggling with this issue?

9. Read each of the following passages. In your own words, what does each passage tell us about why God is worthy of our "fear," our honor, and our respect?

   a. Deuteronomy 10:17

   b. Psalm 91:1–2, 4

   c. Proverbs 5:21

d. Proverbs 16:4

e Isaiah 6:1–4

10. The Bible teaches that we receive benefits when we fear God. Complete the chart below by reading each of these verses and briefly noting the benefit it describes.

Scripture Verse	Benefit
Psalm 34:7	
Psalm 128:1	
Proverbs 1:7	
Proverbs 9:10	
Proverbs 16:6	
Proverbs 19:23	
Proverbs 22:4	

Now, which one of these benefits means the most to you? Why?

OUR FEAR: HIS LOVE

11. Read Joshua 1:9. In your own words, restate God's answer to our fear.

12. God described himself to Moses in Exodus 34:6–7 and to the apostle John in 1 John 4:17–18. Reflect on these two passages.

> The Lord, the compassionate and gracious God, slow to anger, abounding in love and faithfulness, maintaining love to thousands, and forgiving wickedness, rebellion and sin. (Exodus 34:6–7 NIV)

> God is love. When we take up permanent residence in a life of love, we live in God and God lives in us. This way, love has the run of the house, becomes at home and mature in us, so that we're free of worry on Judgment Day—our standing in the world is identical with Christ's. There is no room in love for fear. Well-formed love banishes fear. Since fear is crippling, a fearful life—fear of death, fear of judgment—is one not yet fully formed in love. (1 John 4:17–18 MSG)

How does knowing what God is like help you to overcome fear and live more confidently? Be specific.

OUR FAITH: HIS FAITHFULNESS

13. According to Psalm 56:3–4, what are we to do when we're afraid?

14. Read the following verses, then list some practical ways we can demonstrate our trust in God.

   a. 2 Corinthians 10:3–5

b. Ephesians 6:10, 14–18

c. Philippians 4:6

d. Hebrews 13:6

15. Have you used any of these methods to battle fear in the past? Which one(s)? Were they effective? Why, or why not? Which one(s) will you begin to implement in your life today? What results do you expect?

Lesson Two

ENVY

Selected Scriptures

Has envy ever wrapped its ugly green tentacles around your heart? You insincerely smile at your neighbor when she tells you they're putting in a swimming pool. You grudgingly nod your head in agreement when your co-worker tells you she's getting a promotion. You half-heartedly clap your hands as the announcer calls out someone else's child's name for the coveted athletic award. To the outside world, you seem "fine," behaving just like everyone else. But on the inside, you're secretly seething with resentment toward others because of their successes. The green-eyed monster grabs every one of us at one time or another.

The writer of Proverbs tells us, "A heart at peace gives life to the body, but envy rots the bones" (14:30). Envy, left unchecked, sours our hearts with bitterness and damages our relationships. The apostle Peter warns us that envy and other sins like it can keep us from becoming spiritually mature (1 Peter 2:1–3).

So the question remains; how can we deal with envy? First, we need to clearly understand what envy is and where it comes from. Then we can begin to leave envy behind, moving closer to becoming the women God intended for us to be.

ENVY IS A SIN

1. Read 1 Corinthians 3:1–3. What did the apostle Paul designate as a major hindrance to spiritual maturity?

2. Define the word *envy* in your own words. Now, brainstorm at least five or six other words that describe *envy*. As you answer, try to think of the practical ways that envy creeps into your life.

3. Skim over Galatians 5:19–21. Observe the other sins listed alongside envy. Does it surprise you that envy is included in the same list as these other sins? Why, or why not? What does this imply about the seriousness of envy?

ENVY CAUSES COMPETITION AND DIVISION

4. Skim Genesis 29:16–30:24. What did Rachel have that Leah wanted? What did Leah have that Rachel wanted?

5. How did they go about getting what they wanted?

6. How did their envy affect their relationships with each other, with their husband, and with other family members? Please explain.

7. Make a list of some of the types of things we envy in others. Which ones do you struggle with the most? Why are these so tough for you to overcome?

8. Author Mary A. Kassian describes the danger of envy well:

> The problem with envy is that it warps our perspective. When we perceive others to have an advantage over us, we subconsciously feel the need to "level the playing field." We attempt to make up the difference by puffing ourselves up and pulling them down. Like birds, we splay out our own feathers and peck at our opponent's eyes. (*WomenToday Magazine* online)

Consider each of the pairs of people below. What might it look like if they were to try to "level the playing field" with one another? Imagine specific spoken words, actions, or scenarios.

   a. A stay-at-home mom vs. a working mom

   b. A married woman vs. a single woman

   c. A mom whose kids are home-schooled vs. a mom whose kids go to public school

Have you ever actually experienced one of these "rivalries"? What happened? If you could change your response to the other person, would you? Why, or why not?

HOW TO DETOX FROM ENVY: ETERNAL PERSPECTIVE

9. To envy is "to feel resentful and unhappy because someone else possesses or has achieved what one wishes oneself to possess or to have achieved" (Dictionary.com). According to Ephesians 1:3, what do we, as believers, possess?

10. Make a list of the spiritual blessings Paul describes in Ephesians 1:4–14. Now, take some time to meditate on one of the spiritual blessings you've experienced. If you're struggling with envy, how does this spiritual blessing compare with the object of your envy—the person, item, or advantage you have been wanting?

11. In 1 Corinthians 12:12–28, Paul explained how we are to view each other.

   a. What does Paul remind us? (12:12–13)

   b. What does Paul expect us to know? (12:18, 27–28)

   c. How did Paul challenge all believers to relate to one another (12:26, see also 13:4–7)?

d. How do you think viewing one another as 1 Corinthians 12:12–28 describes will help to rid us of envy? Explain.

12. Read Ephesians 4:1–7, 11–16. What happens when a woman rids herself of envy?

What did Paul mean when he said, "We will be mature in the Lord, measuring up to the full and complete standard of Christ?" (Ephesians 4:13 NLT). Take time to look through a few commentaries or other helpful Bible study resources such as those on www.bible.org, www.biblegateway.com, or www.biblestudytools.net as you form your answer.

Read 1 Samuel 20. Why do you think Jonathan *wasn't* envious of David? Remember, Jonathan was the natural heir to Israel's throne!

What, if any, disparity exists between our understanding of God's sovereignty and our tendency to struggle with envy?

HOW TO DETOX FROM ENVY: EARTHLY PRACTICE

13. Galatians 5:26 states, "Let us not become conceited, provoking and envying each other." Read each Scripture passage below. A woman who has rid herself of envy is (or can):

    a. Romans 12:15

    b. Romans 14:19

    c. 1 Thessalonians 5:11

    d. Galatians 5:22–23

Read Galatians 5:16–26. What exactly does it mean to "walk by the Spirit?" What kinds of things does Paul promise we will *stop* doing if we choose to walk by the Spirit? What kinds of things will we *start* doing?

14. Have you ever encountered a woman who wasn't envious? If so, what was she like? What helped you to notice that quality in her? How did she treat others? Please share a bit about the way she impacted you personally.

15. Write Proverbs 14:30 on a note card, and place it somewhere you will see it often. When you find yourself struggling with envy, remind yourself of its consequences. When you come back to the group next week, be open about your struggles with and victories over envy.

NOTES AND PRAYER

Lesson Three

INADEQUACY

Selected Scriptures

Consider this insight from Scottish pastor William Arnot:

> To every true Christian these two things may be said: "You have need
> of Christ and He has need of you." The simple fact that a Christian is
> on earth and not in heaven is proof that there is something for him here
> to do. (As quoted in Pritchard online)

Do you believe that God has a special purpose for your life? Or have feelings of
inadequacy caused you to doubt your value to God and to others? Perhaps God
is calling you to do something that you fear may be beyond your ability? Maybe
nagging thoughts of your own insufficiency have hindered you? Insecurity is a
painful place to be.

You are not alone. Many people in Scripture were called by God to do something
significant, but they too struggled with their own sense of inadequacy. The best
way to fight feelings of inadequacy and insecurity is to develop a healthy sense of
confidence in God and in ourselves. Then we can be fully mature Christians, useful
to the cause of Christ in this world.

HUMBLE BEGINNINGS: MOSES

At God's direction and through His enablement, Moses led more than two million people out of Egypt, across the Red Sea, and through the barren wilderness to the border of the Promised Land. He also authored the first five books of the Bible. Yet Moses did not start off believing in his own greatness . . . quite the contrary.

1. Skim Exodus 3 and 4. What obstacles or insecurities caused Moses to feel inadequate for the task to which God had called him? How did God respond to each one?

Moses's Obstacle	God's Response
3:11	3:12
3:13	3:14
4:1	4:2–9
4:10	4:11–12
4:13	4:14–16

When God had answered all of Moses's concerns, what did Moses do? (See 4:18.)

2. Consider each of the issues below. Which one(s) cause you to feel the most inadequate? Why?

_____ Lack of credentials: "Who am I?"

_____ Lack of faith: "Who are you, God?"

_____ Lack of credibility: "Who will believe me?"

_____ Lack of talent: "I can't speak."

_____ Lack of courage: "Lord, please! Send someone else."

a. Now, take this issue before the Lord and ask him to help you understand its origin and the way(s) it manifests itself in your life.

b. What one action do you need to do (or not do) and what one truth must you believe (or not believe) in order to overcome this issue? If you are comfortable enough, share your answers with your group.

HUMBLE BEGINNINGS: GIDEON

God gave Gideon an enormous task—to rescue Israel from the ruthless and oppressive Midianites. But there was a rather large catch. God asked Gideon to command an army of 300 men against an army of 135,000! In other words, he wanted Gideon to do the impossible. Let's just say that Gideon, like Moses, wasn't very confident at first.

3. Skim Judges 6 and 7. According to Judges 6:12, how did the angel of the Lord greet Gideon? How did Gideon respond? (See 6:13.)

4. Consider verses 12–15. Contrast the way God viewed Gideon with the way Gideon viewed himself.

5. What was God's answer to Gideon's self-doubt? (See 6:16.) Compare this with God's answer to Moses in Exodus 3:12. What did God promise to both men?

6. Reread Judges 6:34–40; 7:9–11. How did God prove to Gideon that he was indeed with him and would use him to accomplish something significant? Are you surprised that God chose to interact with Gideon in such a tangible way? Why, or why not?

7. Have you ever felt like Gideon—like the least likely person to succeed or to do something significant? Why? Is there something in your family background or upbringing that causes you to feel this way? How does his story encourage you? Please share.

 Skim 1 Samuel 16–17. Compare and contrast what you've learned about Moses and Gideon with David and his encounter with Goliath. How did David feel before he conquered the giant? In other words, how do you think he developed such confidence in God and in himself? Taking a cue from David, how could you develop a history with God, so that you will be able to respond confidently when he calls you to do something for him?

HUMBLE BEGINNINGS: PAUL

Paul, the great apostle, authored more than half of the New Testament. But unlike Gideon, Paul had every earthly reason to be confident in himself. He had the right pedigree, the right education—all the right credentials (Philippians 3). Yet God allowed something to come into Paul's life that caused him to feel very weak and inadequate. Though we're not sure exactly what afflicted Paul, most scholars believe that he suffered from some kind of physical ailment because he described it as "a thorn in my flesh" (2 Corinthians 12:7).

8. Read 2 Corinthians 12:7–10. According to Paul, why did God allow him to suffer from this problem?

9. How did Paul respond to this issue at first? Then, after he realized that God intended for him to endure the "thorn," how was Paul able to overcome this obstacle and press on with what God wanted him to do?

10. Are you dealing with a "thorn" like Paul's? Has some physical or emotional problem caused you to feel inadequate, insecure, or inferior? What is it? How does Paul's example encourage you?

WHAT GOD WANTS FOR US

God has significant plans for each one of us (Psalm 139:16; Jeremiah 29:11). Sometimes they seem impossible in our eyes, and we feel inadequate for the things he calls us to do.

11. Read John 15:8, 16. Summarize these verses in your own words. What kind of "fruit" does God intend for us to grow in our lives? (See Galatians 5:22–23.) Why is it important that we "bear fruit"?

12. Has God called you to do something that you feel is beyond your ability? What is it? To forgive someone? To put a stop to some habitual sin? To love someone who is difficult? To share your faith? To start or lead a particular ministry? Explain.

WHEN GOD ASKS US TO DO THE IMPOSSIBLE

13. Read the following verses. God has given us tools to enable us to purge the toxin of inadequacy and accomplish something significant for him. In your own words, what are they?

    a. Matthew 28:19–20

    b. John 16:13–15

c. 2 Corinthians 3:4–6

d. Philippians 4:13

Read Psalm 121:1–2. Now look up the word *help* in a Bible dictionary. (You can obtain one in a Christian bookstore or find one online at www.bible.org, www.biblegateway.com, or www.biblestudytools.net.) Paraphrase the definition in your own words. Then look up five verses in which the word *help* is used and brainstorm at least one practical, personal application from each verse.

WHAT WE MUST DO

13. Read Hebrews 11:32–39. What enabled ordinary people to do extraordinary—even impossible—things for God? Circle the correct answer from among the choices below.

Talent   Personality   Wealth

Faith   Education   Physical strength

Using a Bible concordance, look up the stories of each person mentioned in Hebrews 11. How did God use each one to accomplish his purposes? What did each person's faith look like in a practical sense? Brainstorm ways that you can develop and exercise this kind of faith.

14. Were all of the people mentioned in Hebrews 11 successful in the world's eyes? Why, or why not? What makes someone successful in God's eyes? (See Hebrews 11:39.)

15. Read Philippians 3:3–8. What does Paul warn us against placing our confidence in? What does Paul's warning mean to you, personally?

16. In light of this lesson, what does a healthy sense of confidence in God and in yourself look like? You may describe situations, list adjectives, draw pictures—be creative.

detox

Lesson Four

PEOPLE-PLEASING

Selected Scriptures

"What will people think?"

"Will they like me?"

"What if they don't?"

Do you find yourself asking these questions often? Do you frequently consider other people's opinions before you make decisions about what to do, where to go, what to wear, what to say, or even how to think? Do you ever compromise your own values and standards in order to gain approval from others? Do you need constant affirmation and the assurance that you are lovable and acceptable? Do you allow others to determine your personal sense of worth and value?

We all feel the need to please others. In a sense, that is a normal part of living with our friends, family, neighbors, and so on. But when our people-pleasing goes too far—when we become overly sensitive to the opinions of others and work to meet those expectations—we will damage our spiritual growth, our personal relationships, and our inner sense of peace and joy. But how can we have a healthy understanding of whom we are to please? Scripture provides the answer.

THE NEED TO PLEASE

The toxin of people-pleasing can be defined as "the extreme desire to gain and keep the approval and acceptance of others." If we don't have a healthy understanding of our own worth and value as God's beloved children, apart from who other people think we are and expect us to be, then we naturally place inordinate pressure on ourselves to perform. This pressure, these unreasonable expectations, will lead to imbalance and perfectionism in our relationships, our work, our attitude toward our appearance—essentially everything we are and do. We lose ourselves, becoming people we're not for the sake of impressing those we want to please.

But why? Why are we willing to give up so much of ourselves to please someone else? Our underlying motive in all of this is fear. We're afraid that if we don't measure up to other people's expectations, then we will disappoint them and they will reject us. Secretly we're terrified that we don't have what it takes to be loved and accepted for who we really are.

WHO WE REALLY ARE

1. Read Ephesians 1:4–6 and 2:10. According to these verses, describe who we are.

2. Write Ephesians 2:10 in your own words, adding in your name (where appropriate).

3. What are some of the things God has called of us, as believers, to do? Read Matthew 22:37–38, Acts 1:8, and 2 Corinthians 1:4 for some ideas.

4. If God has created you for a purpose, what does that tell you about your worth in his eyes? Do you really believe you are important to God? Why, or why not?

WHO WE SHOULD PLEASE

5. Read John 8:28–29. Whom did Jesus seek to please? From what you know of his life and ministry, how did his choice affect his words and actions?

6. Read Acts 5:17–42.

   a. When faced with the choice to please (obey) the authorities or to please God, whom did Peter and the apostles choose (5:29)?

   b. What happened to them as a result (5:18, 40)?

c. Did they regret their choice (5:41–42)?

d. Describe a time when you were faced with a similar choice—to please God by doing the right thing in the face of adverse consequences or to please people who were pressuring you to do something you knew was wrong.

7. The apostles were frequently in trouble with certain people for preaching the gospel. Read 1 Thessalonians 2:3–6. When are you most tempted to use flattery or put on a mask in order to please people or to obtain their praise? Please share.

8. Read the following verses. Why should we seek to please God rather than people?

a. 2 Corinthians 5:8–10

b. Galatians 1:10

c. Revelation 4:11

WHAT PLEASES GOD

When we love someone, we naturally want to please that person. God desires an intimate, loving relationship with each one of us. And our desire to please him should ultimately grow out of our love for him. Ephesians 5:10 instructs us to "find out what pleases the Lord." However, sometimes we struggle with the unhealthy fear that we cannot do enough to win (and keep) his approval. Because we know he is perfect, we tend to think he requires perfection. But this perspective could not be farther from the truth. He loved us so much in our imperfection that he sent his only Son, Jesus Christ, to die for our sins. And through the person and work of Jesus, we are made perfect in God's eyes. (See Romans 5:8–9.)

So, understanding that we are his beloved, valued children, how can we please him?

9. The disciples essentially asked the same question. How did Jesus respond in John 6:28–29?

10. Read Hebrews 11:5–6. Why do you think faith is the primary foundation for pleasing God?

11. God's children, living by faith, can and do please him. Look up the following verses and briefly restate each one in your own words.

a. Psalm 69:30–31

b. Philippians 4:14–18

c. 1 Thessalonians 4:1–7

d. 1 John 3:21–23

WISELY CHOOSING TO PLEASE PEOPLE

In the early church, tension grew between Jewish Christians and Gentile Christians. Jewish believers felt constrained by the dietary laws and sacred days prescribed by Moses in the Old Testament. The Gentile Christians felt no such constraint. The apostle Paul, a Jewish Christian, addressed this issue in the church.

12. Read 1 Corinthians 10:23–33. According to Paul, why is it wise to please people on occasion? When does he say this attitude is appropriate?

13. Brainstorm several real-life situations where it might be appropriate to limit our freedom in order to please others.

14. If we choose to please people, what should our motive be (see Romans 15:1–3)?

15. What are some wrong motives for wanting to please people? Try to list at least five.

16. Which of these do you struggle with the most? Why?

A TIME FOR PLEASING OURSELVES

17. Read Philippians 2:3–5. Keeping these verses as well as the 1 Corinthians passage in mind, how would you describe a proper balance between pleasing God, pleasing others, and pleasing ourselves?

18. What could you do to become more of a God-pleaser than a people-pleaser? Come up with three or four practical suggestions. Put a star by the idea you will you put into practice this week.

Lesson Five

BIBLICAL ILLITERACY

Selected Scriptures

"The grass withers, the flower fades, but the word of our God stands forever"
(Isaiah 40:8). "Your word is a lamp to my feet / And a light to my path"
(Psalm 119:105). "If you continue in My word, then you are truly disciples of mine;
and you will know the truth, and the truth will make you free" (John 8:31–32). As
the very words of the almighty Creator-King of the universe, Scripture is our priceless treasure. As the divinely inspired guide to a godly life, the Bible is our timeless
resource. As the ultimate, absolute truth in a confused, searching world, God's
Word is the foundation for all we are, all we do, and all we say.

So if the Bible is all of these . . . if Scripture is priceless, practical, and true, then
why don't we spend time reading it, much less doing what it says? Why don't we
spend time with Jesus in his Word?

Are we just lazy? Studying is hard. It requires effort, time, concentration, and
persistence. Have we tried to study the Bible but failed to understand what it says?
Have we struggled to find anything in it that seemed to apply to our lives? Or do
we just not know how to go about "getting into the Word"?

What if we could know how to study God's Word for ourselves? What if our study
becomes fruitful, and we come to know Jesus more intimately and learn how to
live life well? Would we be more motivated to spend time, energy, and effort on his
Word? Let's learn how to study the Word; how to know God's ways, understand
him more fully, and "continue to enjoy [his] favor" (Exodus 33:13 NLT).

LOOKING FOR LIFE-CHANGE

The Word of God is active and living (Hebrews 4:12). Scripture has the power to transform our lives, to draw us into intimacy with our Savior, and to teach us how to live well. The apostle Paul communicated this to his friend Timothy when he said, "All Scripture is inspired by God and is useful to teach us what is true and to make us realize what is wrong in our lives. It corrects us when we are wrong and teaches us to do what is right. God uses it to prepare and equip his people to do every good work" (2 Timothy 3:16–17 NLT).

In this lesson, we will work with two different methods for studying the Bible. After briefly looking over both of them, please select *either* the Devotional Method or the Probing the Passage Method. Then, proceed to implement the method of your choice this week.

THE DEVOTIONAL METHOD

The goal of devotional study is to select a passage and meditate on it, seeking to understand both its meaning and how it should impact your life. You may want to spread the steps of this method throughout your week. In other words, pace yourself, and allow the Holy Spirit time to illuminate the Word of God in your heart.

Each of the following passages speaks to the value, use, or impact of God's Word. Please select one of the following to use as you work through the Devotional Method of study.

Psalm 119:9–11

Proverbs 30:5–6

John 17:15–18

Hebrews 4:12–16

Choose your own: _____

Step One: Pray for insight about how to apply the selected passage to your life.

> The Psalmist prayed, "Open my eyes to see wonderful truths in your instructions" (Psalm 119:18 NLT).

Step Two: Meditate on the verse(s) you have chosen to study.

Meditation is basically the careful digestion of a thought. Read a passage and then think about it over and over again; "Scriptural meditation is reading a passage in the Bible, then concentrating on it in different ways" (Warren 34).

You may meditate on a passage in several ways:

Visualize the scene. Try to place yourself into the biblical situation. Who is there? What does it sound like, feel like, smell like, or taste like? What's happening? What do you see? Imagine that you are the person involved in the story/passage.

Emphasize different words in the passage, and notice the subtle shifts in its meaning. For example, if you are studying Matthew 24:35 where Jesus said, "Heaven and earth will disappear, but my words will never disappear" (NLT), try the following:

"Heaven and earth will disappear, but **my** words will never disappear."

"Heaven and earth will disappear, but my **words** will never disappear."

"Heaven and earth will disappear, but my words will **never** disappear."

Read different translations. Read the verse(s) in different translations like the New Living Translation (NLT), the New International Version (NIV), the New King James Version (NKJV), or The Message (MSG). Notice the different English words used to translate from the original languages and try to piece together a fuller understanding of the verse(s).

Paraphrase the passage. Write out the verse(s) in your own words.

Personalize the passage. Insert your name (where appropriate).

Step Three: Using the insights you discovered during your meditation, come up with an application for the verse(s). Your application should be personal and practical—something specific and clear.

The **SPACEPETS** acrostic can help you create your application. Each letter represents a question that addresses a possible angle for application within your verse(s). As you read the verse(s), do you see a . . .

Sin to confess?

Promise to claim?

Attitude to change?

Command to obey?

Example to follow?

Prayer to pray?

Error to avoid?

Truth to believe?

Something to praise God for?

Step Four: Memorize a key verse from your passage.

Now that you've completed your Bible study using the Devotional Method, consider the following questions.

1. Did the Holy Spirit reveal any personal and practical application(s) to you as you studied your passage? If so, what were they?

2. What did you think of the Devotional Method? Did you enjoy a particular aspect of it?

3. Previously, what has hindered you from getting into God's Word? Why do you think you've struggled with this obstacle? Brainstorm two or three practical ways that you might overcome this issue and begin to study God's Word regularly.

THE PROBING THE PASSAGE METHOD

The goal of the Probing the Passage Method is to use inductive study to discover what God desired to communicate to the original audience and then to us today. This discovery happens as we bombard the text with many types of questions. In a sense, learning to study the Bible begins with asking the right kinds of questions!

Please use Luke 10:38–42 as you work through this method of study.

Step One: Prepare.

Read Luke 10:38–42 several times this week. Pray, and ask the Holy Spirit to illuminate this passage for you.

Next, read the introduction page to the book of Luke in any study Bible or basic commentary. Discover who authored the book, when he wrote it, who he wrote it to, and why he wrote what he wrote.

You may also want to read the passage in different translations. (For example, you might choose the New International Version (NIV), New American Standard (NAS), The Message (MSG), New Living Translation (NLT), or the New King James Version (NKJV). Each one takes the original language and translates or paraphrases it into English. Some focus on a word-to-word translation, others use a phrase-by-phrase approach, and still others focus on making the English easy to read in modern terms. Reading the passage in a variety of versions will help you to understand its true meaning.)

Step Two: Observe.

What do you see?

Simply look at what the author is saying. Many questions will come to mind as you read and reread the passage. Ask them, and be sure to write them down.

Observe the facts. Try to visualize yourself in the story.

Who?

Identify all the "who's" in this passage? For example: Who's talking? Who's listening? Who's there? Who are the characters?

What?

Identify the action. To do so, list all the verbs or actions performed by the characters. What is being said? What is happening?

When?

When did/does the action take place? What is the sequence of events?

Where?

Where does the passage occur? Where are the characters? Where did they come from? Where are they headed? Identify all of the locations or places in the passage.

Why?

Why did the author write this passage? What was his point? Are there any cause and effect relationships in the passage?

How?

Do you notice any feelings or emotions being expressed in the passage? What important details do you observe? What descriptive words (adjectives and adverbs) are used to further clarify the meaning? What is the atmosphere or tone of the passage?

Identify key words. Look for words (and their synonyms) that are repeated in the passage.

Consider the definition of each key word. You might choose to write your own based on the passage or to look up the word in an English dictionary or a Bible dictionary. (Bible dictionaries are available online at www.biblegateway.com or www.biblestudytools.net.)

Record any other observations. What other details do you observe in this passage? Any comparisons or contrasts? Any metaphors or images?

Step Three: Interpret.

What does the passage mean?

Now that you have gathered all sorts of facts and clues like an investigative reporter, it's time to move to the next step: interpretation. When you interpret the passage, you are really answering questions about its meaning. Why does the author say what he says? And what did his words mean to the original audience? What do they mean to us today?

Ask yourself "why" questions:

Why did Luke place the account of Mary and Martha (10:38–42) right after he wrote about the greatest commandment (10:25–28) and about how to be a good neighbor (10:29–37)?

Why did the author use two women to tell this particular story?

Why did Martha get upset?

Why did Mary sit and listen?

Why did the author choose to tell this story?

Other questions:

Ask yourself "what does it mean" questions:

What did it imply when Mary sat at Jesus's feet?

What general principles can you see in Jesus's reply to Martha?

What did this episode mean to the disciples?

What did it mean to the original audience for whom the author wrote?

Other questions:

 Research the significance of Mary's position at Jesus's feet. (You can find resources at www.biblegateway.com, www.biblestudytools.net, www.bible.org, or at your local Christian bookstore.) What does Mary's position tell us about Jesus? About us? Explain.

Step Four: Apply.

What does the passage mean to *me*?

Now that you have observed and interpreted the passage, the next crucial step is this: *So what?* It's time to move from seeing and understanding to doing, to applying God's Word to our lives. In this step, we let the knowledge move from our heads down to our hearts; we act on what we've learned.

How did Luke expect his original audience to respond?

How does this passage apply to you, your family, your job, your desires, or your attitudes?

Ask yourself:

Is there a truth I need to believe?

Is there an example I need to follow?

Is there a promise I need to accept and trust?

Is there an attitude I need to change?

Is there an action I need to take or avoid?

Is there a sin I need to confess or forsake?

Is there a verse I need to memorize?

Is there something I am to be encouraged by?

Now that you've completed your Bible study using the Probing the Passage Method, consider the following questions.

1. Previously, what has hindered you from getting into God's Word? Why do you think you've struggled with this obstacle? Brainstorm two or three practical ways that you might over- come this issue and begin to study God's Word regularly.

2. Share the insights you discovered as you studied Luke 10:38–42. What did you apply to your life from this passage?

3. What did you find beneficial about this method of study?

Lesson Six

SIN

Selected Scriptures

If our American culture could be summed up in one sentence, it might be Frank Sinatra's classic lyric, "I did it my way." According to George Barna, ninety-two percent of Americans declare themselves to be "self-sufficient" (Barna.org). Independence is and always has been the American ideal. We admire and aspire to be the "self-made" man or woman. We count those who "pull themselves up by their bootstraps" as heroes. And we feel entitled to certain "rights"—to be happy all the time, to have everything we want, to do what we want to do when we want to do it, and to say what we want to say, anyplace and anywhere.

But does the decision to go our own way and live independently really help us to become spiritually mature, confident women? Absolutely not. Instead, the Bible teaches that independence from God leads to sinful, selfish living. Adam and Eve chose to go their own way, and look what happened! (See Genesis 3.) By refusing to surrender to God's command, they were removed from the Garden of Eden, from God's presence, and from the eternal life he intended for them. Instead of freeing themselves; they found themselves enslaved to their own desires, powerless to control their urges. They plunged the whole human race into a long history of rampant self-indulgence.

What God wants for us, what he has always wanted, is a fully restored, intimate love relationship with each one of us—one that allows us to grow into fully mature, Christlike women. He wanted it so much that he sent his son to die for us, to pay the penalty for our sin, and to release us from its power. The last thing God wants is for us to return to the prison of sin.

So why do we cling to our sin? Why do we keep on doing the things from which God himself has freed us? How can we learn to let go of the sin that keeps us from growing into the women God has always meant us to be?

THE WAY WE WERE

In the beginning, Adam and Eve enjoyed an open, intimate relationship with God in the Garden of Eden. He was holy and righteous; they were pure and innocent; and they walked together often, enjoying each other's company. God gave them freedom, in a broad and generous way, to enjoy the garden's abundance. But he did warn them with a single, simple instruction, in order to protect them: "From the tree of the knowledge of good and evil you shall not eat, for in the day that you eat from it, you will surely die" (Genesis 2:17). However, they disobeyed him; they sinned. And their sin had the devastating consequences of guilt, shame, pain, loss, suffering, death, destruction, and much more. Worse, their sin separated them from God, and they had to leave his holy presence (Genesis 3:24).

We bear both the heritage and the consequences of Adam and Eve's sin. Sin has also separated us from God. We are sinners by birth, by nature, and by choice (see Romans 1–3).

THE WAY WE ARE

1. God has designed and put into action a specific plan in order to restore our relationship with him. Read John 3:16–18 and 1 John 4:9–10. Briefly outline this plan in your own words, paying special attention to our role in it.

2. When we believe in Jesus, we are changed. According to Ephesians 4:24 and 1 Peter 1:3, how are we different?

3. In 2 Corinthians 5:14–17 we learn that we have a new identity. Using your own words, describe who you are in Christ. Thinking through the verses in the previous question as well as this passage, how have you changed since you trusted Christ?

4. Read the following verses, and note some phrases that describe us as Christians. Which of these means the most to you right now? Why did you choose this particular verse?

   a. Romans 1:6

   b. Romans 5:1

   c. Romans 8:16

   d. Colossians 3:12

   e. 1 Thessalonians 5:5

5. Read Romans 6:1, 5–8. What has changed about our relationship to sin? Can you think of a time in your life when you recognized that a particular sin had lost its power over you? How did this realization affect your spiritual growth? Please share.

OUR CALLING

6. Read 1 Peter 1:14–16 and 1 Peter 2:9, 11. What kind of people has God called us to be? And what is God's purpose for us as Christians?

7. Look up the words *holy* and *sanctified* in both an English dictionary and in a Bible dictionary. Summarize the meaning of each word in a single sentence. In reference to the verses above, do you think God expects us to lead perfectly sinless lives? Why, or why not?

8. We know that God has called us to be holy and obedient daughters. What has God provided to help us? (See 1 Corinthians 6:19; 2 Peter 1:3–4.)

OUR RESPONSIBILITY

9. Read Genesis 3:1–6. In your own words, what motivated Adam and Eve to sin?

10. According to Romans 7:5 and Galatians 5:16–17, why do Christians continue to sin, even though we have already been forgiven (see also Colossians 2:13)?

11. What are some of the ways that Christians rationalize their pet sins?
    NOTE: A "pet sin" is a sin we purposefully choose to keep around. In other words, we *know* we are violating God's Word, but we do it over and over again anyway.

12. Consider a sin that you keep in your life even though you know it violates God's Word. Reflect back on Genesis 3:1–6. What motivates you to continue in your pet sin? Can you let it go? Will you let it go? Why, or why not?

13. Think through and describe the ways in which your pet sin might be hindering your spiritual growth. (For help, see John 8:34; Romans 6:12–13; 7:17, 20, 23.) Do you feel a tension between who you want to be and the sin that tempts you? Explain.

14. In 2 Samuel 11, King David sinned. God sent the prophet Nathan to rebuke him in 2 Samuel 12:7–10. Now, take a look at John 16:7–8 and Hebrews 4:12. How are we convicted of sin?

15. How did King David respond to God's rebuke? (See 2 Samuel 12:13; Psalm 51:1–4.) Given David's example, how should we respond when the Holy Spirit convicts us of sin?

Look carefully at 1 John 1:6–10. Using a dictionary, look up the words *confession* and *repentance*. What part do you think confession and repentance play in cleansing us from sin? Think through the meaning and implications of each action as you answer.

16. What should we do when we are tempted to sin once again? Note the helpful instructions or examples in each of the following verses.

    a. Psalm 1:1–2

    b. Psalm 119:11

    c. James 1:21–22

    d. 1 John 2:28

    e. Other: _____

17. "Therefore, since we are surrounded by such a huge crowd of witnesses to the life of faith, let us strip off every weight that slows us down, especially the sin that so easily trips us up" (Hebrews 12:1 NLT). Remember the pet sin that you mentioned earlier? What do you need to do in order to "strip off" this sin and start doing things God's way?

Lesson Seven

DISTRACTION

Selected Scriptures

Have you ever seen someone driving down the road talking on her cell phone, flossing her teeth, and putting on make-up—all at the same time? Your first thought is to get out of her way, isn't it? Why? Because she is dangerously distracted! She can't focus on her driving because she is doing so many other things. Have *you* ever been the distracted driver? We've all been guilty at one time or another.

Researchers at the University of Utah have found that drivers using cell phones, even with hands-free devices, experience a decrease in the ability to process peripheral vision, creating a potentially lethal "tunnel vision." This "inattention blindness" slows reaction time by twenty percent and resulted in some of the test subjects missing *half* of the red lights they encountered in simulated driving. "We found that when people are on the phone, the amount of information they are taking in is significantly reduced," says associate professor David Strayer. "People were missing things, like cars swerving in front or sudden lane changes. We had at least three rear-end collisions." (Charny, CNET.com)

Do you sometimes feel that you are "missing things" in your spiritual life? Perhaps you have a kind of "tunnel vision" that prevents you from seeing the big picture of life? Have you developed an "inattention blindness" because of the distractions in your life? Distractions are everywhere. And they come in so many forms!

The Bible has much to say about where to focus our attention so that we don't get off course in life and miss important things, especially in our relationship with God. So, turn off your cell phone, turn off the TV, forget about the dishes in the sink, and *focus*!

WHAT'S IN A WORD?

1. Look up the word *distract* or *distraction* in the dictionary. List some of the distractions in your life that tend to draw your attention away from Christ.

2. Read the parable of the sower in Mark 4:3–20.

   NOTE: Jesus's parables are stories from ordinary life that are meant to illustrate spiritual truth. This particular parable illustrates what happens when God's Word is "planted" in different kinds of soil—with the soil representing the condition of the heart.

   a. What were some distractions that "choked the Word" when it was planted in thorny soil? (See Mark 4:18–19.)

   b. Which of these distractions applies the most to you? How does it affect you?

   c. Jesus addressed worry and wealth as specific distractions in Matthew 6:19–34. What is his solution to dealing with these issues? Now, look back at verse 33. What does he say about where our attention should be focused?

   d. What is the ultimate effect of distractions on our spiritual growth? (See Mark 4:19.)

Read the story of Hannah in 1 Samuel 1. What burden or desire distracted Hannah from fully worshipping the Lord? Do you think her burden/desire was wrong in any way? How did she handle it, and what was the result?

WHERE SHOULD OUR FOCUS BE?

3. In Philippians 3:15, Paul writes that those who are mature should have a particular view of the Christian life. Read Philippians 3:7–15 and briefly summarize the passage in your own words.

4. What was Paul's focus—his one great passion?

5. As he matured as a Christian, Paul developed some settled convictions.

   NOTE: The word *consider* is used three times in this passage. Paul uses it to imply a sense of settled conviction.

   We could rightly infer that Paul's convictions led to his singular focus in life. List them here.

6. What were the specific items that Paul considered to be "loss" or "rubbish" in comparison to Christ? (Refer to Philippians 3:4–7.)

7. What items or issues in your life should you consider to be "loss" and "rubbish" in order to fully follow Christ? Be specific.

8. In Philippians 3:14, Paul refers to the Christian life as a race—a race we're running in order to receive a heavenly prize. With this in mind, look back at verse 13. What did Paul do in order to focus on the prize?

9. In a practical sense, how can you work to forget the past and focus on what lies ahead? Brainstorm at least three actions you can take or truths you can memorize.

STAYING FOCUSED

10. Staying focused on Christ and his Kingdom can seem nearly impossible in the midst of all the distractions of this world. Paul offers us some wise advice in the book of Colossians. Read Colossians 3:1–17.

    a. In the first two verses, where does he encourage us to focus our thoughts?

b. Make a list of the earthly things where we tend to set our hearts and minds. Next, make a list of the heavenly things we should be focusing on. (Consider the things you love, the things you think about, how you spend your time, where you spend your money, and so on.)

Earthly Things	Heavenly Things

c. Compare the lists. How much time and mental energy do you spend on each category?

d. What does this tell you about where your focus really is?

e. How can we stay focused in our actions, attitudes, and motivations?
(See Colossians 3:5, 16–17.)

f. Refer back to 3:1, 3–4. What helps us to stay motivated in this process?

14. As a way to summarize this lesson, describe how your life would be different if you were able to become more and more focused on heavenly things.

Lesson Eight

DISAPPOINTMENT

Selected Scriptures

dis·ap·point·ment (noun)

1. A feeling of sadness or frustration because something was not as good, attractive, or satisfactory as expected, or because something hoped for did not happen

2. The failure to attain somebody's hopes or wishes

Synonyms: dissatisfaction, discontent, disillusionment

Antonym: satisfaction
(Dictionary.com)

"Life just hasn't turned out like I thought it would." Does that thought visit your mind often? Do you live in a state of disappointment? Do you feel like you've missed the life you should have had? We've all given up dreams along the way. Many things haven't turned out to be as fun, as satisfying, as successful, or as worthwhile as we expected. At one time or another, we've all borne the burden of disappointment, the pain of disillusionment, and the frustration of discontent.

But we don't have to live in the valley of disappointment. God offers us abundant life, a life of great satisfaction and joy in him.

UNMET EXPECTATIONS: A BIBLICAL PERSPECTIVE

Moses, the patriarch, was used by God to free the Hebrews from bondage and to lead them to the Promised Land (see the book of Exodus). The hand of God was evident throughout his life in amazing, jaw-dropping ways. To mention one, he was born at a time when the Pharaoh had declared that all Hebrew boys were to be killed. His mother chose to defy the order and placed Moses in a basket in the river. Incredibly, the basket was found by the Pharaoh's daughter, and she decided to raise Moses as her son. A condemned Hebrew boy, Moses was now a child of the house of Pharaoh.

1. Describe what you think Moses's life was like as a prince of Egypt. What expectations do you think Moses had for his future?

2. Read Exodus 2:14–21. Describe Moses's life after he killed the Egyptian.

3. Do you think Moses might have struggled with great disappointment at this turn of events? Put yourself in Moses's shoes at that time. How would you have felt?

Turning to another biblical account, in Luke 24:13–27, we read of two people who came to Jerusalem with great hopes that Jesus would set their nation free from Roman oppression. Their expectations of the Messiah were shattered when Jesus died on the cross. And though they had heard of the empty tomb, they had not seen the risen Christ. So, three days after Christ's death the two decided to go back home. During their walk back home, Jesus came to them.

4. What expectations did they have? (See Luke 24:18–24.)

5. In your own words, why were they feeling disappointed (24:17)?

Next, let's consider the book of Ruth, a true story about the transformation of two women from emptiness to fullness, from poverty and fear to security and hope.

6. Read Ruth 1. Do you think Naomi's life turned out like she thought it would? Explain.

7. The name Naomi means "my joy" or "sweetness." However, in 1:20, she refers to herself as "Mara." Mara means "bitterness." Whom do you think Naomi was bitter toward?

8. In your opinion, how did Naomi view God?

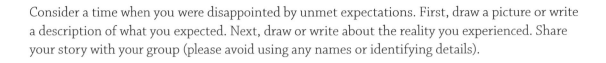

UNMET EXPECTATIONS: A PERSONAL PERSPECTIVE

Consider a time when you were disappointed by unmet expectations. First, draw a picture or write a description of what you expected. Next, draw or write about the reality you experienced. Share your story with your group (please avoid using any names or identifying details).

Now, make a list of the expectations you currently have for your life. Think about your friendships, health, marriage, faith, career, family, children, and so on.

DEALING WITH DISAPPOINTMENT

Let's go back to the people we've met so far in Scripture and look at how each one of them dealt with disappointment. Their lives reveal much about how God intends for us to deal with our own unmet expectations.

9. The men on the road to Emmaus were deeply disappointed that Jesus wasn't who they expected him to be (Luke 24:13–24).

   a. What did Jesus say to them about their disappointment (24:25)?

   b. Read Luke 18:31–33. Before his death and burial, what did Jesus say to his disciples?

   c. In Luke 24:27, what did Jesus do to correct their expectations and to help them understand his true nature and mission?

10. The expectations held by the two men on the road to Emmaus didn't line up with God's Word. Can you think of a time when your expectations about life (faith, health, marriage, career, children, parents, and so on) didn't line up with what the Bible said? What happened? Did you struggle with disappointment in relation to that issue? How did you deal with it?

11. What else did Jesus do to encourage the two men (Luke 24:29–31)? What do his actions tell you about how he will respond to your disappointment?

Look back at the list of expectations you created on page 84. Using one of the following methods, explore what the Bible has to say about our unmet expectations. For example, if you have unmet expectations related to your family, look up what the Bible has to say about family. If your unmet expectations fall under another category, look up that issue.

- Look online at www.biblegateway.com under the "Topical Index" section. Search under the issue you selected. You'll receive a myriad of possible resources and related Scripture passages.

- Use the concordance in a study Bible to look up verses regarding the area of your expectations.
  NOTE: A concordance is a study tool that lists words exactly as they are written in Scripture and lists the key passages that contain those words.

- Use the topical index in a study Bible to find references pertaining to your topic.

- Take a look at the biblical passages you unearthed. How do your expectations line up with Scripture? Drawing from what Scripture says pertaining to your topic, what should your expectations be?

12. Read Exodus 3:1–10. What happened to Moses while he was living in the desert? After his earlier disappointment, do you think he ever imagined that God would choose to use him for such an incredible task? Why, or why not?

 Research the meaning of God's name as given in Exodus 3:14. What do you think God was revealing about himself to Moses? How might knowing God's true identity help us in dealing with our own disappointments? Explain.

 Read the book of Ruth in one sitting. Take some time to write about Ruth's experiences in a first-person, modern-day story. Focus on the different ways God provided for Naomi and Ruth by thinking through all the ways God has provided for you and for others that you know.

13. In Psalm 73, the Psalmist is disturbed because he observed that those who *didn't* follow God seemed to be living better than those who *did* follow God. Skim 73:1–22. What emotions did the Psalmist express in verses 21–22?

14. Now, read Psalm 73:23–28. In your own words, explain what changed the Psalmist's heart?

15. Read these six verses once more. Ask the Holy Spirit to make God's Word real in your heart. Which section of this truth do you need to internalize in order to better deal with the disappointments and unmet expectations in your life?

Meditate on these words from Max Lucado about David, the Psalmist: "[He] has found the pasture where discontentment goes to die. It's as if he is saying, 'What I have in God is greater than what I don't have in life'" (30). Pray, and ask the Lord to help you find satisfaction in him, because he is greater than anything you could possibly have in your life!

detox

Lesson Nine

UNFORGIVENESS

Selected Scriptures

On October 2, 2006, a gunman walked into an Amish schoolhouse near Lancaster, Pennsylvania, and mercilessly shot ten young girls, mortally wounding five of them. Ten precious lives were just beginning, then some were cruelly stolen and others forever changed. Twenty parents were faced with pain most of us, thankfully, can't begin to fathom. Would we have expected them to rage against the deceased gunman and his family? Definitely. Would we have expected them to be angry at the God they serve, questioning his love and justice? Certainly. And we would have understood their reaction. But these grieving parents, as well as the entire Amish community, offered immediate words of forgiveness and reconciliation (CNN.com). They also acted on their forgiveness, establishing a charitable fund to help the *gunman's* family. The world was literally stunned, speechless at the unfathomable grace on display.

Forgiving people who have hurt us is hard. Sometimes it feels like an impossible task. Everything in us wants to hold our offender hostage. We want to withhold from them whatever it is that they value. We want revenge. We want them to pay; we insist they make restitution. And it's still not enough. The hurt still gnaws away at our souls, breeding bitterness, resentment, and anger.

As God's girls, we are called to forgive. In fact, Scripture instructs us to forgive, over and over again if necessary, because unforgiveness is toxic to our souls. In opposition to our human sense of fairness, unforgiveness always holds *us* hostage rather than the one who offended us. It halts our spiritual growth, keeping us from becoming all that we can be.

But we can let go of unforgiveness with God's help. And when we forgive, we become vivid displays of the forgiveness God has so generously given to us. Let's start the process of releasing our unforgiveness so we can move on to becoming the women God designed us to be.

UNFORGIVENESS DESTROYS

God longs for us to be free from an unforgiving spirit, because refusing to forgive will destroy every one of our relationships. Our marriages, friendships, and even our relationship with God are all vulnerable to the weeds of bitterness, anger, and resentment that will grow in the fertile soil of an unforgiving heart.

1. In his book, *The Gift of Forgiveness*, Charles Stanley defines forgiveness as "The act of setting someone free from an obligation to you that is a result of a wrong done against you." He goes on to say that forgiveness involves three elements: "injury, a debt resulting from the injury, and a cancellation of the debt" (16). List some of the reasons why we might refuse to cancel someone else's debt to us.

2. Read Galatians 5:19–23, 25; 6:7–8. How do you think unforgiveness hinders our spiritual growth? Explain.

3. According to Ephesians 4:31–32 and Hebrews 12:14–15, bitterness often lies underneath the inability to forgive. In what ways do you think bitterness "grows up to trouble you, corrupting many?"

4. The resentment bred by unforgiveness has a way of spilling over into other relationships. Think of a time when someone's bitterness towards someone else spilled over onto you. What happened? Were you hurt? How did you respond? (If you choose to discuss this question in your group, avoid sharing names or specific details.)

Read Matthew 6:14–15. Explain what Jesus meant when he said, "If you refuse to forgive others, your Father will not forgive your sins" (NLT). As you work through this question, be sure to consult a reliable study Bible and a few Bible commentaries.

FORGIVING OTHERS

We will all experience rejection or hurt at one time or another. Therefore, we will all have to deal with the issue of forgiveness. And in that moment when someone wrongs us, we have to decide what to do with our hurt. Will we hold our offender hostage until he or she meets our demands? Will we withhold our love, service, and kindness until we feel like we have been repaid for the wrong done to us? Soon, we will have to decide if we will let our hostage go or hold on tightly, opening the door to the consequences of unforgiveness. In choosing to let go, we find ourselves becoming free—free to become more like Jesus.

5. In Colossians 3:13, what are we instructed to do for those who wrong us? Why do you think we have been given this command?

6. Now, read Romans 3:23–26 and Hebrews 9:22, 26. Summarize what God did in order to forgive us.

Do a biblical word search for *forgiveness*. You can do a word search by going to www.biblestudytools.net, clicking on the online study Bible, typing in the word *forgive* or *forgiveness* in the "search" box, and then looking through the Scriptures that come up. Now, create a thorough list of words or phrases that describe God's forgiveness.

7. Read Matthew 18:21–33. What did Peter ask? How did Jesus respond? In your own words, what was the point of the parable?

 Read the story of Joseph in Genesis 37–45.

a. Consider how Joseph's brothers responded to their father's rejection.

b. Consider how Joseph handled the rejection and cruelty of his brothers.

c. Consider what Joseph's view of God looked like during the years of his bondage. (For help, see Genesis 39:21–23.)

d. Consider the process by which Joseph reconciled with his brothers.

Drawing directly from this section of Scripture, how would you advise a woman who is struggling with unforgiveness? How would you lead her through the process?

8. According to the following verses, what else can we be assured of when we forgive? What does this assurance mean to you?

a. Genesis 50:19–20

b. Romans 12:19–21

9. Are you currently struggling to forgive someone? How did you get hurt? What does the relationship look like now? How might your newfound understanding of God's forgiveness help you to extend forgiveness to this person? Please share, but if you're answering in your group, avoid names and specifics.

THE PROCESS OF FORGIVENESS

Author and pastor Charles Stanley has simplified the process of biblical forgiveness into five key steps (127–131):

- Recognize you've been totally forgiven.

- Release the person from the debt you believe is owed you for the offense. This must be a mental, emotional, and sometimes even a physical action.

- Accept the other person as he or she is, and release him or her from the responsibility to meet your needs.

- View the other person as a tool of growth for you.

- Make reconciliation.
  NOTE: Reconciliation usually involves re-establishing contact with another person. However, not all relationships should be re-established. Use discretion!

Remember, forgiveness is a process that begins with an act of your will, a choice to obey God's command and to forgive. However, don't be discouraged if the process is hard, lengthy, and painful. God is faithful and will honor your obedience.

FORGIVING OURSELVES

Too many times, we struggle to forgive others because we haven't fully trusted in God's forgiveness for us. We spend our time walking around feeling guilty for the sins we've committed. We say to ourselves, "How could God forgive me? What I have done is awful." God longs for us to believe him; to settle the issue of our forgiveness once and for all so that we can move on toward what he has for us.

NOTE: Be careful of the distinction between guilt and conviction. In the classic book, *The Search for Significance*, Robert McGee explains it well:

> Although Christians are free from guilt, we are still subject to the conviction of sin. The [Holy Spirit] directs and encourages our spiritual progress by revealing our sins in contrast to the holiness and purity of Christ. . . . [But] His conviction of believers is not intended to produce the pangs of guilt. Our status and self-worth are secure by the grace of God, and we are no longer guilty. Conviction deals with our behavior, not our status before God. . . . While guilt is applicable to non-believers and originates from Satan, conviction is the privilege of those who believe and is given by the Holy Spirit . . . [leading] us to the beautiful realization of God's forgiveness and the experience of His love and power. (144)

10. Read Romans 8:1. Look up the word *condemnation* in the dictionary. Now, rewrite this short verse in your own words. What was Paul communicating to us as believers?

11. Read King David's words in Psalm 103:3, 10–14. List as many reasons as you can that we have to be free from guilt and condemnation. Then take a moment to meditate on this list, thanking God for his love and forgiveness. Allow any residual guilt in your heart to fall away. You are forgiven and free!

12. According to Hebrews 10:22, what is Christ's sacrifice able to do? Why was it so effective? (See Hebrews 10:17–18.)

13. If God doesn't bring up our sin anymore, then who does? (See Ephesians 6:16.)

14. Pastor Charles Stanley states, "Being forgiven has nothing to do with feeling forgiven. Being forgiven has to do with what God did for us" (139). Read 1 Peter 5:8–9. When we feel guilty about our past sins, what should we do?

15. Brainstorm some ways we can battle Satan's attacks—especially those dealing with guilt and condemnation. Now, read John 8:32; Philippians 3:9–10, 12–15. Add to your list any other ideas these verses bring to mind.

16. If you struggle with listening to the "father of lies" (John 8:44) regarding this issue, take time to write out a prayer of trust, claiming the truth about Jesus's provision for your sins. Don't forget to thank God for what he's done!

BIBLIOGRAPHY

"Amish Grandfather: We Must Not Think Evil of this Man." CNN.com. October 5, 2006. Retrieved from http://www.cnn.com/2006/US/10/04/amish.shooting/index.html on May 27, 2007.

Barna, George. "Self Descriptions." Barna.org. Retrieved from http://www.barna.org/FlexPage.aspx?Page=Topic&TopicID=34 on June 16, 2007.

Charny, Ben. "Does Cell Phone Use Blind Drivers." CNET.com. January 27, 2003. Retrieved from http://news.com.com/Do+cell+phones+blind+drivers/2100-1033_3-982325.html?tag=item on June 16, 2007.

"Disappointment." Dictionary.com. Retrieved from http://dictionary.reference.com/browse/disappointment on June 16, 2007.

"Envy." Dictionary.com. Retrieved from http://dictionary.reference.com/browse/envy on June 16, 2007.

Holman Illustrated Bible Dictionary. ed. Chad Brand, Charles Draper, and Archie England. Nashville, Tenn.: Holman Bible Publishers, 2003.

Kassain, Mary. "Green with Envy." *Woman Today Magazine*. Retrieved from http://womentoday-magazine.com/selfesteem/envy.html on June 12, 2007.

Lucado, Max. *Traveling Light*. Nashville, Tenn.: Thomas Nelson, 2001.

McGee, Robert S. *The Search for Significance*. Revised and expanded edition. Nashville, Tenn.: Thomas Nelson, 1998.

McManus, Erwin Raphael. *The Barbarian Way: Unleash the Untamed Faith Within*. Nashville,Tenn.: Nelson Books, 2005.

Nelson Study Bible: New King James Version. ed. Earl Radmacher. Nashville, Tenn.: Thomas Nelson, 1997.

Pritchard, Ray. "You Will Be My Witnesses: God's Job Description for Every Christian" sermon from the series "The Adventure Begins (Acts 1)," March 15, 1998. Retrieved from www.keepbelieving.com/sermons on June 16, 2007.

Stanley, Charles. *The Gift of Forgiveness*. Nashville, Tenn.: Thomas Nelson, 1991.

Warren, Rick. *Personal Bible Study Methods*. Pastors.com, 1997.

Made in the USA
San Bernardino, CA
14 February 2015